GARDENER'S MAGIC
and Other
Old Wives' Lore

BY THE SAME AUTHOR
WITH
MAUREEN BOLAND

Old Wives' Lore
for Gardeners

GARDENER'S MAGIC

&

Other Old Wives' Lore

Bridget Boland

THE BODLEY HEAD
LONDON SYDNEY
TORONTO

© Bridget Boland 1977
ISBN 0 370 30053 X
Printed and bound in Great Britain for
The Bodley Head Ltd
9 Bow Street, London WC2E 7AL
by W & J Mackay Limited, Chatham
Set in Monotype Ehrhardt
First published 1977

The decorations have been chosen from a number of
sources including the 1521 and 1533 editions of
the *Hortus Sanitatis* (pages 9, 21, 23, 43, 52, and
54) and Gerard's *Herball*, first published in 1597
(pages 16, 51, 56, and 61).

CONTENTS

Remembering
Maureen

FOREWORD

What is the magic of old gardens? Can it be in part that those who designed them had another object in mind besides that of pleasing the eye, which tends to be our only criterion? Perhaps plants had more personality, more dignity, more mystery, when they were held in respect, even in awe, because of the wonderful powers they were supposed to possess. A garden that has nothing in it but the showier hybrid tea and floribunda roses followed by a blare of dahlias and chrysanthemums has no such sense of the mysteries of nature, of plant and gardener interrelated in the scheme of things. Something of the old magic can be recaptured in a garden planted today with some awareness of the old lore. Even if one has no urge to experiment with the occult possibilities of the herbaceous border, there is much pleasure in looking at the demure faces of some of the humblest plants, once thought so potent, and paying a lingering respect, as to kings in exile, to those who have seen better days.

When my sister and I were sifting material for our book on Old Wives' Lore we had reluctantly to put aside a lot that we hated not to pass on but had to admit did not fulfil the requirement that we had set ourselves, that the advice should be practical, however eccentric. I have drawn on that surplus for this book, which is really as much about gardeners as gardening; for gardener's magic is about the hopes and fears of men, in love or loveless, terrified or inquisitive, always in trouble of some kind or other, who looked out into the garden for help—and perhaps found it, because they were so sure it must be there.

Whether the long history of magic proves the suggestibility of man, or the wisdom of believing in what has been experienced but not yet explained, is immaterial: magic *is* fascinating, it *does* enchant. The scientists who recently discovered the existence of particles of matter and named them Charms, because almost all they knew about them was the way they affected their neighbours, should be given a Nobel Prize for nomenclature.

There are plenty of books about the recognised medicinal virtues of plants, so of these I say nothing here: this book is about their magical powers pure and simple, and I make no claims for them that can be contested under any Consumers' Protection Acts. Because a great deal of the advice is indeed guaranteed to be of absolutely no practical use at all, it is interlaced with some additional down-to-earth old wives' lore, much of it kindly sent to me by readers of our first book, which is very practical indeed. It is hoped there will be no confusion between them.

(8)

FOR LOVE

Food for Lovers

The Doctrine of Signs (that every plant bears some mark of the use to which it can be put) is very important in gardener's magic. 'Behold', says Paracelsus, 'the Satyrion root, is it not formed like the male privy parts?' No one can deny this. Accordingly magic discovered that it can restore a man's virility and passion. The lupin and carrot were, though to a lesser degree, considered aphrodisiac for the same reason, as were Shakespeare's 'long purples', that botanists call *orchis mas* but 'liberal shepherds give a grosser name'.

'Periwynkle when it is beate to a poudr with worms of ye earth wrapped about it and with an herbe called houslyke,' says an early translation of a Book of Secrets attributed to Albertus Magnus, 'induces love between a man and his wife if it be used in their meals.' As so often with magic one

(9)

wonders how the strange virtue of these humble ingredients in combination came to be discovered. The difficulty of wrapping a worm round some powder would seem considerable; but the great Albert was probably no cook. The ingredients are easily grown, the houseleeks on roof tiles or in any crack or cranny in a wall, and periwinkles in any shady corner, particularly if it is a little damp.

In the same shady corner can be grown sowbread (*cyclamen napoletanum*), sometimes found in wild woodland and easily made happy with a little leafmould. Gerard says that 'Sowbread, being beaten and made up into trochisches, or little flat cakes, is reported to be a good amorous medicine to make one in love, if it be inwardly taken.' That splendid Renaissance lady, Caterina Sforza, who captured castles and held Cesare Borgia at bay and knew as much about love as war, held that sowbread did wonders for a woman's looks—which may explain the efficacy of the other recipe as well. Culpeper, in the seventeenth century, maintained that the roots of *asparagus saturis*, boiled in wine and 'taken fasting several mornings together, stirreth up bodily lust in man or woman, whatever some have written to the contrary.'

'Our gallants' "sweet powder",' writes Evelyn, is made chiefly of 'the white and dotard (decaying) part' of the ash. The white dead nettle, whose leaves are delicious cooked in butter, was

thought lucky for lovers (if not aphrodisiac) because in the flower, if you hold it upside down,
the stamens can be seen lying for all the world
like two people side by side in a curtained bed—
whence its name Adam-and-Eve.

Love Potions

The spreading of Islamic culture in the middle
ages, particularly after the coming of the Moors to
Spain, brought much Arabian magic to Europe
and from as far away as Persia, including a potion
to make one in love. It was compounded of cloves,
laurel seeds, Italian thistle and sparrow-wort,
drunk in pigeon broth. The Arabs also recommended the annointing of the male member with
pyrethrum and ginger in lilac ointment, and the
female parts with balm of Judea.

Spring water in which willow seeds have been
steeped was strongly recommended in England
as an aphrodisiac, but with the caveat that he who
drinks it will have no sons and only barren
daughters.

The Lovers' Bedchamber

A bridal bedchamber, we are advised, should first
be fumigated with burning leaves and fruit of the
bramble as a magic protection against any evil
wished upon the couple by disappointed rivals.

The fumigation should be performed well in advance, for the windows of course must not be opened lest the virtues of the smoke drift out, and the odour of burning brambles is not of the pleasantest. This would have been counteracted in older times by the strewing of sweet-smelling herbs on the rushes on the floor, those considered best for the bridal chamber being verbena, marjoram and meadowsweet, mint, thyme, valerian and violet, all sacred to Venus, and basil and broom, sacred to Mars. A bowl of pot-pourri containing them could be placed on a table by the door instead. It should be stirred, we are told, with the fourth finger of the left hand by anyone coming in, to release the scents and induce the mood of love.

The sheets of lovers should be perfumed with marjoram—Virgil says that when Venus carried

off Ascanius to the groves of Idalin she laid him on a bed of it, and she should know.

Pillows stuffed with verbena were recommended for their strong aphrodisiac scent; but strong is the word, and a sprig of it thrust in among the down of the modern pillow might well suffice.

At the bedhead should be hung, that surest of all talismans for lovers, a piece of mandrake root. The mandrake's roots derived their magical properties from the Doctrine of Signs, for it resembles the human form; but it grows wild only in eastern Mediterranean countries, and was difficult and expensive to obtain. Those who wanted the talisman were therefore warned to beware of substitutes, for roots of the native bryony could, with a little adaptation, be made to resemble it and were often sold at fairs as the real thing. Lovers were also warned not to take powdered mandrake roots internally, for it has a narcotic quality (indeed, too much of it can send one to sleep for ever), and even a little of it will induce a drowsiness which will defeat its purpose in the bridal chamber.

When we remember that beds were canopied and curtained against the draughts, the couple with their scented sheets and pillows and their talismans would be cosily prepared for love indeed.

Precautions

Understandably, perhaps, when all marriages were 'arranged' and the attentions of the spouse must often have been singularly unwelcome, mediaeval herbalists were much concerned to provide anti-aphrodisiacs as well. Hildegard of Bingen, a twelfth-century nun, gives counter-potions against the effects of the mandrake, of which she passionately disapproves. One involves picking seven shoots of broom and the roots and leaves of one cranesbill and two mallows, which were then pressed and rubbed and mashed (using the middle finger only) in a mortar till they formed a paste that could be spread on a cloth and bound to the body, which would nullify the power of the mandrake completely.

Arabian herbalists advise as anti-aphrodisiacs a decoction of henna flowers, or of onions with egg-yolk and camel's milk, or of chick peas and honey.

Other magical herbs apparently had more permanent effects: a woman who drank salvia cooked in wine would never conceive; nor would she if she ate a bee.

When infidelity is suspected, we are assured, certain precautions can be taken against the lovers by the spouse. Plutarch says that white reeds, picked just before sunrise in a river, and strewn in the wife's bedroom, will drive the

adulterer mad and make him confess. Male
chauvinist that he was, he evidently took it for
granted that the wife would be the erring partner.
To keep a wife from erring when he is away,
Arnold of Villanova (early in the fourteenth century) advises the husband to hide two halves of an
acorn in the pillow (as was done by magicians
hired by defeated rivals to inhibit conjugal love).
But he kindly adds that the lovers can counteract
the long-term effects at any rate of this by putting,
if they can find them, the two halves together,

keeping them for six days, and then eating half each.

When love, who laughs at locksmiths, has made a mockery of magic too, and even the most careful of spouses fear themselves deceived, the mandrake is summoned to the rescue again. It is then that a mild decoction of the powdered root might save the breaking heart with a night's oblivion. Shakespeare doubted it. The Moors in his day were credited with knowing more of magic than anyone, and Desdemona's father, for one, certainly believed that Othello had won her love 'with some mixtures powerful o'er the blood' or other occult arts. But once the seed of doubt of her fidelity is planted in Othello's brain, Iago can safely whisper as he watches him:

> *'Not poppy nor mandragora*
> *Nor all the drowsy syrups of the world*
> *Shall ever medicine thee to that sweet sleep*
> *Which thou ow'dst yesterday.'*

Practical Old Wives' Lore

The Soil

I hate the use of the word 'soiled' to mean indiscriminately 'dirty'. Soil is clean and it is beautiful, and hands (and boots, too) covered with it are only as they should be. I love to get my hands in the earth on a warm day and feel how live it is—as live as any flower or animal, it almost pulses. I love to feed it, and my conscience, which sometimes stops me buying plants I want, can never get a word in edgeways when it is a question of buying manure.

People say poultry manure is too hot, because they can't be bothered to treasure it long enough —keep it for two years, in a heap with alternate layers of wood-ash, and there is nothing better.

A compost heap is also a lovesome thing, God wot. In our twenty feet by twenty feet garden in London (where I had a very small heap and was forever poking among it in search of the 'red flat-tailed lobworms' which the books said it should produce, and my worms never seemed particularly red and their tails were sort of pointed), it appeared to me that potato peelings took far longer to rot than the rest, and even to slow down the whole heap. I took to keeping them separately in a wooden crate alongside, where they rotted splendidly in no time. I found that delicious goo oozed out between the slats, so I kept a tray under part of it that could be slid out like a drawer, and, diluted with as much water, made a fine liquid fertiliser. The hessian bags that some plants come in from nurseries, filled with a little animal manure from your heap and kept in a bucket of water by it, make a lovely liquid manure, too.

A correspondent told me how, in her childhood in Scotland, the family used to complain that her mother lavished more food than she ever gave her offspring on the marrow she was growing for a prize, in fierce competition with the episcopalian vicar of a neighbouring parish, and that the vicar, with the aid of prayer, was in a stronger position than she was anyway. Her mother won the prize, and remarked: 'Prayer is all very well, but there's nothing to beat the best minced steak.'

A more sinister story was told me about another vicar, who could never be induced to part with the secret of how he grew such fabulous roses, until finally some ladies of the parish cornered him and bullied it out of him: 'I bury a cat under each bush,' he said.

TO PROTECT THE
GARDEN

If a garden always expresses in some way the
mind and spirit of the gardener, is it too fanciful
to believe that something of the peace we find in
old gardens comes from steps that its makers took
to ensure it? Every care was taken to see that no
evil should enter. The summoning of dark forces
for our own purposes is all very well, but no one
wants the occult blowing about where it listeth
out of control.

Occasionally on entering a very old walled
garden you will see over the door a horse's head
carved in stone. This is the relic of a belief that
dates from Roman times. 'Some have used to put
in the garden the skull of a mare or she-ass that
hath been covered,' wrote Topsell in 1607, 'with
the persuasion that the garden will be fruitful,'
and Pliny was even of the opinion that it also kept
out the caterpillars. A 'physic garden' would
sometimes have carved over the door the ancient
sign for secrecy, an open rose with two buds
above it, to preserve the secrets of the herbalist's
art.

In the crevices of walls houseleeks were en-
couraged, to protect the garden's luck and also to
keep out lightning.

If in digging deep the modern gardener

should turn up a very old earthen pot, it may mean that someone took the advice of Pliny, and buried a toad in it against storms and hail.

The ancients planted the laurel against lightning—a sure protection, the thirteenth-century Bartholomew assures us. If the laurel is found darkening the house, however, it is more likely to have been planted by Victorians to prevent the neighbours looking in or, like an uncle of mine in Ireland, to prevent the servants wasting their time watching people playing tennis in the garden. To credit trees with magical powers seems pleasanter.

The trees themselves were felt to need protection too. A good Christian monk, the thirteenth-century Abbot of Beauvais, advised the hanging of coral in an apple tree to defend it against all weathers. Probably one of the little pieces that form a natural cross would have been his choice. Others suggest that when the apple is planted the name of Asmodeus, the devil who tempted Eve (unless you believe it was the she-devil, Lilith), should be written on the earth and cancelled with a cross. Cider used to be poured over the roots of apples as a libation and the poet Herrick records the custom of drinking to the health of all fruit trees on Christmas Eve:

> '*For more or less fruits they will bring*
> *As you give them wassailing.*'

On the oak, sacred tree of the Druids, the Celtic sign of the circle divided into four equal parts used to be carved for protection (lest it fall), long after Druidic worship had been forgotten.

In the same way some old-fashioned gardeners will still always grow a certain plant 'for luck', having forgotten the original significance of the magic: verbena, for instance, that was held by the Saxons to be a sure protection against storms and hail, as the ninth-century Leechbook of Bald and Cild assures us.

Animals in the Garden

Those wise in witchcraft would never allow a parti-coloured animal in the garden, such as a tabby cat or a black-and-white dog. This tabu probably derives from Genesis XXX and XXXI, in which parti-coloured animals are regarded as unclean. The modern gardener may find it easier to ask his neighbour to keep his dog or cat under better control by claiming such a superstitious view as this and getting a reputation for mere eccentricity, than by saying the creature is badly trained, and being considered offensive. The tabu did not apply to birds, luckily, except the magpie, which does rather flaunt its challenge.

Those who had beehives were advised to hang juniper inside them against adverse magic, and to 'rub all within with fennel, hyssop and tyme flowers, and also the stone on which the hive shall stand' (Gervase Markham), for this will make the bees 'love their hive and come gladly home'. This is an admirable example of the giving of magical significance to a piece of sound common sense, for the scouring of the hives with these herbs will clean them and also scent them with herbs that bees do indeed seek out. Bees, by the way, should always be paid for, for while stolen plants (particularly in the case of rue) are said to thrive best, this is not true of bees. And if you are much stung by them do not complain too loudly, for they are known to sting fornicators most.

The owner of a dovecote or pigeon loft was advised to be sure to hang in it the head of a wolf, so that 'neither cats, weasels nor anything that will hurt will enter' (Lupton). As with so much magic, the modern would-be practitioner may find this prescription difficult to follow. Perhaps a fox's mask would do instead.

When Walking in the Garden

It was regarded by French herbalists as unlucky (but fortunately rare) to see an aloe in flower. Except in the evening, when it was fortunate, it was unlucky to see a spider, as it was to see a squirrel at any time. If you saw a spider spinning, it meant that someone was plotting against you. If you saw a cuckoo while it was actually singing, you would be, had been, or were being cuckolded.

Gerard is very specific about what can be divined from oakapples, which 'broken into at the time of their withering, do foreshadow the sequence of the year' to Kentish husbandmen. 'If

they find an ant, they foretell plenty of grain to ensue; if a spider, then, say they, we shall have a pestilence among men; if a white worm or a maggot, then they prognosticate a murrain of beasts and cattle.' Lupton goes further: 'If the little worm doth fly away, it signifies wars; if it creep, it betokens scarceness of harvest; if it turn about, then it foreshadows the plague.'

It has always been considered safe to savour the odours of the garden on the air as you walk, for plants that have evil in them hold it close while they grow; but it was said that you should not on any account lie down to rest under an ivy tree and fall asleep, for it could be the death of you.

Practical Old Wives' Lore

Pests

The ancient writers provide a wealth of advice for keeping out such things as snakes, scorpions and cockatrices, but little for dealing with more common pests; one authority, telling you how to deal with wasps, urges you to tie a thread round the leg of one and follow it as it flies home, and then destroy the nest; and a Victorian writer says that any you find 'may be killed almost instantly by the application of a little sweet oil on the tip of a feather'. To deal with the problem more practically, hang a jar with a little beer or sugared water in it in fruit trees or bushes or in a pergola under which you sit, and let the wasps commit suicide at their leisure.

To get rid of grubs on fruit trees, light your bonfires on the windward side of your orchard; many will curl up and drop off, but they will still be alive, so you must sweep them up and destroy them afterwards.

Many people worry lest the slug bait they buy have ingredients in it poisonous to birds. The safest thing to do is to put a little ordinary bran, or orange peel, on the ground and cover it with a cabbage leaf, pinned down with a twig through it against wind. The slugs and snails will come to the bait and remain happily digesting under the leaf until you come by in the morning, turn the leaf over, and sprinkle them with salt or lime, which will kill them.

Against pigeons, I am told that if you up-end a red bottle on a stick it will deter them. I cannot vouch for this myself, but my friend swears she has proof.

To prevent mice feasting on your newly-sown peas, put holly clippings in the trench. This undoubtedly works.

On the same principle, poke brambles down mole runs, and they will not use those runs again. The trouble is that they will, in my experience, make others. Sink empty beer or lemonade bottles in the runs with the necks just protruding, and the wind will make ghostly noises that will terrify them. The same objection applies; but by the time you have your whole garden wailing like a coven of banshees it is conceivable they may decide the entire area is haunted and it will get a bad reputation in mole circles for generations to come.

You can keep heron out of your fish pond by running a single strand of wire around it, twisted round an occasional stick, about nine inches from the ground. The bird does not land in water but wades into it, and will not be able to step over the wire. It can be as fine as you like, and it need not be unsightly.

One creature you should keep in the garden is a toad. No greenhouse, or cucumber or melon frame, should be without one. It will serve you

well by eating noxious insects, so give it a mate that it may not be bored in its captivity. And do check to see whether it 'wears yet a precious jewel in its head', as Shakespeare says in *As You Like It*.

WORK
IN THE GARDEN

In the Toolshed

The ancients advised that yarrow should always be kept hanging in the toolshed 'for safety'; and it came to be believed that the plant protected the shed from entry by thieves. Here is an admirable example of the good sense often hidden in magic: yarrow staunches bleeding—in France it is known as 'the carpenter's herb'. What better reason could there be for keeping a bunch of it hanging handy in a toolshed? The ancients also advised that it should be bound round the handles of tools for work outside.

When helping in other people's gardens we are sometimes puzzled by the presence of very strange equipment in their toolsheds. I have often been asked the purpose in mine of a piece of bent wire from an old coat hanger on the end of a long pole. It has in fact no more sinister use than exactly fitting my gutters so that I can stroll round the cottage scraping, with no trouble, leaves and pine needles from them.

The magically-minded would keep among their tools the longest possible iron nail, as only an iron nail would serve for digging up certain roots for magical purposes, and it could be a tedious process with a small one. But frequently tools, especially knives, made *without* iron were called for; presumably this dated from very ancient times when iron was regarded as a new-fangled thing and rather vulgar, much as we look upon plastics now, while flint was still respected.

A gold knife or sickle absolutely had to be kept for cutting mistletoe. A bull's horn and a bone were other tools that could be kept for digging when iron must not be used.

Many of these tools have, of course, perfectly practical uses. I realised recently, when trying, without unpicking half a rockery, to move without damaging the roots a plant that had grown too big, that a nicely curved bull's horn was exactly the tool I needed to poke under stones with, and that my toolshed was inadequately equipped.

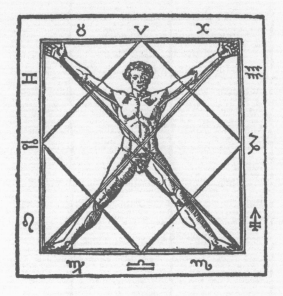

At Work

Great attention has always been paid by gardeners to the phases of the moon; and this not only because it affects the plants but because man himself is wiser (according to Michael Scot in the thirteenth century) when the moon is waxing, and therefore any work that needs thought, such as planning a layout, should be done then. Attention must also be paid to the zodiac, whether sowing, planting or picking a herb, confining the work if possible under a sign auspicious to the plant. Vervain (*verbena officinalis*) for instance, is peculiarly sacred to Venus, as to some degree are any plants used in love potions and the like, and therefore the position of planets needed, it was felt, sometimes to be considered.

All repetitive actions in the garden were better done nine or seven times, or in multiples of these numbers, which are magical in the oldest lore; three has only been magical since the coming of Christianity, as representing the Trinity, and in Christian magic nine is regarded as three times three.

When a plant to be grown is of particular importance, such as the mandrake, the soil thrown up by moles, ants or beetles should be used in preparing the position, or that which lies between cart ruts. It need not trouble the enthusiast in magic that the latter injunction may have originated in someone realising that soil between cart ruts had probably been well manured. For growing plants for love-potions, particularly valuable, according to Pliny, was the soil taken from under the print of your right foot wherever you were standing when you heard the first cuckoo of the year—especially for would-be adulterers, perhaps.

Whoever practised garden magic, whether professionally or for personal use, would find that stocks were constantly being depleted by the demand for roots at inconvenient times of year. All roots that are used in magic, however, can be dried; and presumably the professionals kept a stock, cleaned and carefully labelled. If a client failed to pay for a root, the gardener would replant a portion at once in the same place; for the client's trouble would then continue to grow worse until the cash was handed over.

Sowing Seed

Watching the phases of the moon has always been regarded as particularly important when sowing, which should only be done when it is waxing, not waning. This ordinance is now known to be scientifically justified, but I confess to a sentimental attachment to the notion that the forces involved are magical. Even if the moon has now been danced on by astronauts and is littered with American Space Authority hardware, over my garden (and surely yours too) she still shines enchantment. Besides, the sceptical reader should beware: you never know when the wise men of today may not catch up with the magi.

Certain seeds, the ancients felt, need special care in relation to the moon. 'Mark,' says Holinshed's version of Pliny, 'how many days old the moon was when the first snow fell the winter next before, for if a man do sow rapes and turnips within the aforesaid compass of that time, the moon being so many days old, they will come to be wondrous great and increase exceedingly.' During the twelve years I lived in Rome it only snowed once, and the inhabitants of the City spent their time tobogganing on trays down the steps of the American Embassy; but this is a degenerate age.

Parsley must absolutely be grown from seed, and never, never moved about. Everyone agrees about this. Elinor Sinclair Rhode, in *Herbs and Herb Gardening*, quotes a French saying: '*Repiquer le persil, repiquer sa femme.*' She also quotes old sayings on the difficulty of growing it even from seed: it is so slow to germinate because it goes back nine times to the devil. But if you sow on Good Friday you can prevent this. Never take a house with an established garden in which parsley is not growing, or you will never see the year out. The trouble for the previous owner may have been, of course, the fact that it takes an honest man to grow parsley; or he may have been aware that he who grows it well will have no sons and only barren daughters. All round, it seems safer for a man to make his wife sow it; and indeed there is another saying that where it grows well it is the man of the house who wears the trousers.

Cummin seed is apparently particularly bloody-minded, for when you sow it you should ram it down hard and adjure it not to come up; which it then will.

For Picking

Before picking or digging up, the plant should always be 'saluted' and told for what purpose it is needed, and if possible for whom, thus pacifying it and ensuring its co-operation. Modern investigators who claim that the reactions of plants to being manhandled, or even spoken to harshly, can be scientifically registered, would probably agree that this is a wise precaution. You should spit three times on the piece you pick, and it must never be allowed to touch the ground. There seems to be a feeling that a piece picked off the ground is like carrion, unholy, with the virtue gone out of it. You should never face into the wind as you pick, or look back over your shoulder at the plant after you have done so.

When a plant is to be picked by hand we are warned that it is usually better, and sometimes essential, to do so with the left hand, sometimes even with the thumb and fourth finger of the left hand—the stronger the magic in a plant the fussier it is liable to be. A sixth-century manuscript advises you to hold a mirror over a herb before picking it, before sunrise under a waning moon; you should also be chaste, ungirded, barefoot, and wearing no ring. Modern advice for picking blooms for a flower show is always to do so before the sun is on them, but for magical purposes it is nearly always enjoined that the sun should not have risen at all. In the case of picking from a peony or digging up its root this is absolutely vital, says Pliny, or the woodpecker of Mars is liable to pluck out your eyes.

Some plants require more elaborate rituals than others for their virtues to operate. Thus to use camellia to cure cataract all you need to do is to pick it before sunrise, telling it that you need it 'for the white growth of the eyes'; but for senecio to be effective against toothache you must dig up the root without using iron, touch the tooth with it three times, and then replant it at once; luckily this can be done in daylight, so that it is not necessary for both patient and gardener to be up in the small hours. When picking mistletoe the time does not matter (which is just as well, as it may be difficult enough to climb the tree without having to do so in the dark); but you must sacrifice two bulls beneath first, use your golden knife or sickle, and drop the mistletoe down onto a white cloak stretched out below.

We pick lettuces more often, in the ordinary way, than mistletoe, and probably all too often omit the essential rite of making the sign of the cross over them as we do so. In a book by St Gregory the Great said to have been translated by King Alfred (two surely very reputable authorities) there is a salutary warning about this. A maidservant working in a monastery garden did so, and became possessed by the devil that had been in it. When exorcised, the devil complained that it had been merely 'sitting on the lettuce and she came and ate me'.

The Mandrake

The most elaborate precautions of all have to be taken when digging up the mandrake root; but first a word on how it grows. Too many people think it is as mythical as the phoenix, but its botanical name is *mandragora officinarum var. vernalis* and it can be found wild from Greece, all round the eastern end of the Mediterranean and North Africa, to Spain. The illustrations of it in ancient herbals tend to have been drawn, like those of the rhinoceros or the camel in bestiaries of the same period, by artists who had never actually seen it. In reality it grows like a big rosette almost flat on the ground, with long leaves and very short-stemmed, bluish-purple, cup-shaped, sweet-smelling flowers. The fruits that follow the flowers, and nestle in the heart of the rosette, are yellow and about the size and consistency of a small tomato, unpleasing to the

average palate, but evidently an acquirable taste as the local children are said to enjoy it even to excess, when it causes dilation of the pupils and headache. They normally spit out the seeds, which if swallowed can cause temporary madness followed by catatonic sleep, but are not fatal. The seeds and powdered root were much used in early medicine as an opiate, and by those with Borgia-like tendencies as a poison (though it must have been difficult to administer, not being the sort of thing that could be described as 'tasteless in tea' or, to anyone with an educated palate, in wine). But its chief commercial value seems always to have been as a talisman.

The root does go down exceedingly deep, certainly as much as five feet. The Greeks believed that you might even, if you fell into the hole when you had dug it up, tumble straight down to Hades. Usually we are advised to draw a circle on the ground around it, and some experts prefer the use of ivory or the horn of a bull for this. Some say that the ground should be soaked at intervals for three months with hydromel (one part honey to eighteen parts water, boiled) to 'appease the earth'. Conceivably this may make the operation easier, but the root has now to be dug out without the use of any iron tool. Infinite care must be used not to damage it for it must emerge in the recognisable shape of a man or a woman, and the actual removal should be at sunset. If it is not tugged too violently at the last, it will not give the terrible scream that turns men to stone; but you are advised to tie a dog to the upper part as you lift it so that the evil will go into the dog. Some authorities require elaborate incantations, but others hold that 'In the name of the Lord God of Sabaoth' is enough. The hole should then be filled with sweet fruits or nothing will ever grow there again, which would be a pity for, given its natural habitat, it will have demanded a choice spot in the garden with a full southerly aspect, preferably in a light, sandy soil, for ease of extraction. The root should be treated with every respect and kept wrapped in a shroud, for some say it is the true Origin of the Species of mankind. Paracelsus denies this, but thinks it is not unlikely that a man, or at least an homunculus, may yet be bred from it.

Practical Old Wives' Lore

Sowing

Before sowing very hard seeds that are difficult to germinate, sprinkle them onto a pad of several sheets of wet kitchen paper towels, and keep them on a tray or the lid of a tin, always moist, in a light window until they do germinate, and then wash them off onto the soil.

When preparing a trench for beans, particularly in light soil, line the very bottom with a thick layer of newspaper to retain the moisture. Writers can use rejected manuscripts for the same purpose.

Spraying

Plants that are subject to mildew may with advantage by sprayed occasionally with a decoction of elder leaves. 'Oh wad some power the giftie gie us' of abolishing black spot for aye, but I know none.

Rose Pruning

Don't. Well, not as much as you think you should.

> *'There was an old man of Calcutta*
> *Whose die-back when pruning was utter.*
> *No die-back he found*
> *With tips bent to the ground,*
> *That wily old man of Calcutta.'*

An Indian correspondent of the Rose Society's journal gave this information (in prose). Although we don't have the same climatic problems the advice is good. The reason for pruning is to prevent a plant from growing tall and weak, bald at the bottom with new flowering growth only at the top. If a shoot is pegged right down in January or February, new growth will spring from buds all along its length. Young, whippy shoots should be chosen. It is particularly valuable for old types of roses, for large modern shrub roses, and even for such floribundas as Chinatown and Iceberg. The only drawback that I find is that if the shoot is bent outwards from the base, as is most easily done, the new shoots will be upwards-facing and therefore, when it is released in April, the new growth will be too much crowded on the inside of the shrub. Branches should therefore be chosen that can be poked through and bent *across* the base, so that when it is released the shoots will be on the outside of the plant. Lengths can be cut from opened-out wire coat hangers with a hook bent at the top of each to pin the branches down with.

Picking

One of the best examples of the good sense of old wive's lore is any warning that it is unlucky to pick a certain plant. There is always a good reason, and the fact is that the idea that it is unlucky sticks in simple minds a great deal more easily than the real, varied explanations.

It may be poisonous. You should not pick laburnum for the house because the poisonous seeds, out of the reach of children on the tree, may well be get-at-able in a vase or dropping on the floor.

It may be a plant of medicinal value and should be left growing unless it is really needed: we are told we should always bow to such a plant and apologise if we have to pick from it, explaining why.

It may be a shrub whose next flowers bud from just behind this year's and you will destroy it for a season. In all these cases, Old Wives tell us simply that it is dreadfully unlucky to pick them for decoration, and leave it at that.

FOR THE GARDENER

Not only the garden but the gardener himself was seen by those who practised the magic arts as needing protection, perhaps even more than other men, for he who has skill will have rivals, and he who has power will have enemies. Luckily he did not need to be constantly drinking potions or rubbing on salves for protection, since many herbs were considered effective if just worn or carried about.

An amulet against evil spirits conjured by others could be made of cloth (preferably red) filled with dried betony, peony, and artemisia. Herb bennet was so powerful that 'Satan can do nothing and flies from it', and, as a bonus, the *Hortus Sanitatis*, 1491, says that 'if a man carries the root about with him no venomous beast can touch him'; but I do not know if this is valid for fornicators in the vicinity of beehives, and fear it may only apply to serpents, basilisks, and such.

Dried in a sachet, or even worn as a flower in the buttonhole, the periwinkle (known as Sorcerer's Violet) was by common consent sovereign against any witch not carrying it herself who might come visiting.

A useful string of beads could be made as a charm against all forms of evil out of dried peony roots; they might be carved and fashioned as you would (to make them look innocently decorative), but should not be dyed or painted except with the blue of woad or the yellow of meadow saffron, both protective plants themselves, or the virtue will be sealed in.

The superstitious gardener of today may care to consider the value of ancient advice when he goes out beyond the safety of the protected garden. Hang a root of rhododendron round your neck to preserve you from any savage dogs you may meet. If you are going out to dinner, take some syderica with you as a sure protection from all poisons, particularly (since it bears the image of a serpent on each leaf as a sign) that drawn from snakes.

The surest protection against drunkenness is to wear a wreath of ivy. A woman, of course, if she wishes to conceal that she has any problem in this respect, can always hide the wreath with her tiara. A man can take the alternative precaution of eating five bitter almonds before the meal, which Pliny assures us is effective, and a Roman of his period should know.

Alyssum will prevent anyone getting angry with you, and if you carry heliotrope you can be sure to hear only friendly words spoken. The latter should be wrapped in a laurel leaf with the tooth of a wolf; it should only be picked when the sun is in Leo in August for this purpose, but it can be dried. At a party you expect to enjoy, however, it might be an embarrassment, since no fornicator present will be able to leave until it is removed and you may feel obliged, in common courtesy, to be the first to leave yourself.

To Give Special Powers

Both Bartholomew and the good Bishop Vincent of Beauvais testified that a decoction of heliotrope, drunk with the invocation of powerful enough spirits, had the power to give invisibility at will.

Sometimes invisibility might, apparently, be found not to be enough, and the adept would need to take the form of some other kind of life, and then, to get back into human shape, to bathe in spring water into which anise seed and a laurel leaf had been dropped; if this was not altogether effective (perhaps some trace of the animal form had remained, such as cloven hooves), a strong decoction of the same plants should be drunk.

If the adept, or indeed anyone else, had taken the outward form of an ass, all that was necessary was to eat roses (only the old alba, gallica, centifolia and damask varieties can have been meant when this was written). Perhaps to this day if a donkey is seen eating roses it should, in charity, be left to do so, and not be driven off until it is quite clear that it is *only* a donkey.

For powers of divination, vervain has always been regarded as sovereign. The Romans used it in all lot-casting and prophecy. Heliotrope was also thought helpful for all forms of divination, and today might be particularly useful if the gardener's burglar alarm should fail; for he has only, according to Albertus Magnus, to sleep with it under his pillow to dream a reconstruction of the burglary, complete with recognisable burglar. 'And,' says the rhyme of 'Robin Goodfellow' (1628), albeit with his tongue in his cheek,

> 'Can a magician a fortune divine
> Without lilly, germander, and sops-in-wine?'

Before we mock the superstitions of the past, we should consider some of the preoccupations of our own time. To acquire the ability to see ghosts the Society for Psychical Research should note, carry lavender. It has certainly the most memory-evocative of all scents, and when a garden or room is heavy with it even the least sensitive may feel that round the next corner, or at a turn of the head, anyone who has trod these paths before or crossed this floor might well be seen.

The power to see fairies is more difficult to acquire. They are not at the bottom of every garden. Wild thyme must first be picked 'on the side of a hill where fairies use to be.' The word is 'use', note well, not 'used', so make sure the tradition of their presence is a living one. The injunction comes from a recipe of 1660, which

recommends that you take 'a pint of sallet oyle and put it into a vial glasse; first wash it with rosewater and marygolde; the flowers to be gathered towards the east. Wash it until the oyle becomes white, then put it into the glasse, then put thereto the budds of holly hockes, flower of marygolde, the flowers on tops of the wild thyme, the budds of young hazels. Then take the grasse of a fairy throne [ant hill], then all these put into the oyle in the glasse and sett it to disolve three days in the sunne and then keep it for the use.'

Practical Old Wives' Lore
To Protect the Gardener

I might well pass off as magic (with the addition of an incantation to give it the authentic ring) a fact about the elder bush if it had not been discovered, so far as I am concerned, by so commonsensical a friend: it has an irresistible attraction for flies. If one grows outside your kitchen window, flies will remain happily outside and not come in.

Insects can make the garden a misery to those particularly allergic to their bites. Oil of lavender is sometimes recommended to repel them, but I have found that it too attracts flies, which can be almost equally annoying. The answer is mint, particularly *mentha piperita* (from which menthol is distilled), which repels flies as well as other insects. Rub the face and hands with leaves of it, and it gives the added bonus of a delicious cooling feeling to the skin. Mint or parsley grown on a window-sill is also said to keep flies and insects out of a kitchen; you should bruise the leaves occasionally to release more odour.

That the gardener may not lose friends, he or she should chew parsley before eating garlic.

For the Gardener's Weather Eye

At one time, every well-conducted household contained a copy of *Enquire Within*. An edition published in 1887 was the sixty-seventh, and boasted an issue of one million and thirteen thousand copies to date. It includes some valuable weather lore. The heavier the dew after a hot day, for instance, the more likely is it that the following one will be fair as well, but if there is little dew, and no wind, it will rain. If the moon looks pale or dim, it will rain; if red, it will be windy. If it has been wet or alternatively fine, throughout the period of a moon, it will become the opposite at the change, remain so for four or five days, and then revert to what it was before. If the sky in rainy weather has a tinge of sea-green the rain will get heavier; if there are patches of deep blue, it will become merely showery.

When I was young we were told it would clear altogether if there was enough blue sky 'to make a cat a pair of breeches'.

FOR A MERRY HEART

There are in the old herbals innumerable recipes for what are nowadays called 'heart conditions' (as though the healthy heart were in no condition at all); but there are also many less strictly medical, for the heart as the seat of all our emotions. Is it a hark-back to such ancient magic when pills to calm our anxieties are marketed as Purple Hearts?

Borage provides without doubt the most popular magical herb for the heart. Pliny says it should be called Euphrosinum, so surely does it make a man merry and joyful, and Gerard that, drunk in wine, it makes 'men and women glad and merry, driving away all sadness and dullness'. The modern cocktail-party host who decorates tall glasses of this and that with sprigs of borage surely has no idea how old a practice he indulges in to ensure the success of the evening. Gerard quotes an old saying in dog-Latin which he translates as

> '*I, Borage,*
> *Bring always courage.*'

Like several other herbalists, he also recommended balm and basil drunk in wine.

For the older writers the effects of these herbs seemed purely magical; Paracelsus, on the borderline, considered balm the basis of the Elixir of Life; by Gerard's time medical explanations were beginning to emerge; and it is now understood that balm is an excellent nerve tonic (cheering the

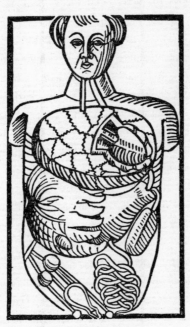

heart indeed). Basil is an even better choice to be taken with alcohol if the party is liable to prove a long one, for it is not only that rare thing, a nerve tonic that is stimulant rather than sedative, but it also settles the stomach, preventing vomiting and nausea. Meadowsweet, according to Gerard, should be boiled in the wine 'to make the heart merry'; and if you make a kind of brandy by distilling the flowers of lily of the valley in it, it will not only comfort the heart but even 'restore speech to those that are fallen into the appoplexie'.

Lest the sceptical modern reader suspect that alcohol is the active ingredient, there is much magic for the heart that does not call for any. Chervil (sweet cicely) roots work wonders 'for old people that are dull and without courage', (Gerard), and marjoram boiled in water 'easeth such as are given to much sighing'. Bartholomew prescribes fumitory: he admits that is is 'an herbe with horrible savour and heavy smell', but 'is natheless most of virtue, for it cleaneth and purgeth melancholy'. You can make the heart merry with 'rosset sweetcakes' of archangel or rosemary flowers baked with sugar, which sound altogether more agreeable.

A purgation of hellebore will 'cheer the hearts of all dull and heavy persons', while one of bugloss is said to be particularly exhilarating for infants. Germander and milk thistle need only be chewed to lighten the spirits. The virtues of

lavender seethed in water to comfort the heart are praised as far back as William Langham in 1579 and as near to our own times as Baron Frederic de Gengins Lassaraz in Paris in the 19th century, who specially recommends it for 'the nervous disorders to which ladies of high birth are subject', poor things.

Personally, I always take the advice of Shakespeare on anything, and he recommends another thistle. 'Go,' says Margaret to Beatrice in *Much Ado about Nothing*, 'get you some of this distilled carduus benedictus, and lay it to your heart. It is the only thing for a qualm.'

FOR CERTAIN PEOPLE

For the Student

You cannot start education too young, as the advocates of pre-nursery schooling aver—but they do not go back far enough: ante-natal clinics should perhaps provide quinces, for it was held in the seventeenth century that 'the woman with child that eateth many during the time of her breeding shall bring forth wise children and of good understanding'. Bugloss is as good for the infant's mind as for his heart. At school, Evelyn says that borage 'will cheer the hard student'. The memory can be vastly improved by smelling or eating rosemary or betony, which indeed are both good for the head generally. 'The flowers of lavender quilted in a cap,' says Turner's Herbal, 1551, 'comfort the brain very well.' Often in old portraits of men of letters they are shown wearing what appears to be a nightcap, and I had always presumed until I read this that it was to impress upon one how studiously they burned the midnight oil; but now I wonder if they were comforting their brains with lavender.

For Athletes

Olympic competitors should check that these aids are permitted by the Committee, but it used to be considered that of value to all athletes were baths in which were steeped mint and balm 'to strengthen the nerves and sinews'. Eating nasturtium was said 'to soften the muscles', but whether this meant to prevent stiffness or cramp or to prevent the ageing athlete becoming musclebound I do not know. The marathon runner should put artemisia and/or camomile in his shoes against weariness in the legs, and also carry a stick, however small, of myrtle for the same purpose. After the race the whole body can be annointed with oil made from nasturtium seeds to 'soften the muscles' again. Any runner will surely benefit from the advice of Webster in *The Devil's Law Case* to one of his characters to eat 'Malaga raisins to make him long winded'.

Practical Old Wives' Lore
Weather-Predicting Creatures

If you find a frog that looks pale yellow, the weather is going to be fine. If it is going to be wet, within hours the same frog will turn dark brown or green. If you hear a cockerel crow long before dawn it predicts rain, or in winter often snow. If the pale brimstone butterfly appears early in the season after a spell of bad weather, it has come out of hibernation because a good spell of fine weather can be expected; later in the season you are liable to see it most just before a change in the weather either way.

The same local sage who gave me these tips says also that a red sky at night (or in the morning) portends sunshine (or rain) only if the sky on the opposite horizon reflects the colour.

A Leech Barometer

The early Victorian encyclopaedia *Enquire Within* contains instructions on how to predict the weather by keeping a leech in a jar, which seems like witchcraft but is not. The country is better drained than it used to be, and you may have to make a journey to the few surviving fens to catch your leech or ask at the kind of chemist's who still spells himself 'chymist', but then you put it in a large jar with three gills of water, changing the latter once a week in summer and once a fortnight in winter. 'If the weather is to be fine, the leech lies motionless in the bottom of the glass; if rain may be expected, it will creep up to the top of its lodgings, and remain there till the weather is settled; if we are to have wind, it will move through its habitation with amazing swiftness, and seldom goes to rest till it begins to blow hard.' If heavy storms are to be expected, 'it will lodge for some days before, almost continually out of the water, and discover great uneasiness in violent throes and convulsive-like motions; in frost as in clear summer weather it lies constantly at the bottom; and in snow as in rainy weather it pitches its dwelling at the very mouth of the phial. The top should be covered with a piece of muslin.'

TO TAKE INDOORS

Against Evils

The magic of the garden, of course, could be used to protect the house as well. Some people still hang up horseshoes outside their door, a relic of the belief that witches feared cold iron; but herb bennet, the blessed, would once have been hung over it inside to keep the devil from crossing the threshold, with betony for the further good of the souls of all within.

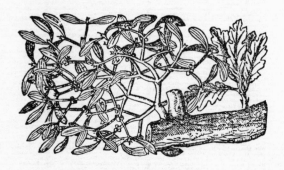

Nowadays mistletoe is brought in only for kissing time at Christmas, but once it hung in every hall all the year round as a sign that guests greeted under it were safe in that house, a recognition of its power, known from Druidic times, to ensure peace and friendship. Other beneficent herbs would be strewed over the rushes on the floors along with such more practical things as pennyroyal (*mentha pulegium*) to deter fleas. If Queen Elizabeth I were coming on a Progress, the wise householder would be careful to strew much meadowsweet, which she was known to value above all, though possibly more for its scent than for its other virtues

To protect the house against the entry of the plague, bunches of rue (herb o' grace) used to be hung at the sides of windows, particularly those facing east, for it is on this side that the infected 'air blows from France'. So powerful was it considered that thieves looting plague-contaminated houses would risk entry if they carried it even if corpses still lay there. Here again we can trace the explanation behind the magic, for though the plague was not airborne it was carried by rats, and rats hate rue.

Our ancestors used also to rub furniture with herbs. The revellers disguised as fairies in Shakespeare's *Merry Wives of Windsor*, after ordering that the elves should strew 'good luck' herbs in every room, decree

> '*The several chairs of order look you scour*
> *With juice of balm and every precious flower,*'

and this not for the scent alone; though alas modern manufacturers who add oil of lavender, probably synthetic, to wax furniture polish have probably forgotten the magic significance of what they do.

Magical Pot-Pourri

Owing to the prevalence of close-carpeting, pot-pourri is probably the most practical way for the modern magic fancier to keep dried herbs in the house, and a far more magical scent will certainly pervade the rooms than that of more conventional kinds. For instance, special bowls of herbs recommended for the bridal chamber on page 12 can be kept in all bedrooms, to which can be added plenty of sweet woodruff, which has the magical property of causing anyone who sleeps near it to dream of summer meadows and wake in a world of new-mown hay even in midwinter. I can find no specific magical use for costmary, (*chrysanthemum balsamita*), but would add it for its scent: in America it is known as Bible Flower (which perhaps sanctifies it), because it smells so sweetly when dried and lasts so long that it used to be pressed between Bible pages and kept there as a bookmarker.

There are, of course, dozens of methods for making pot-pourri, but there is one, devised when magic was taken seriously and therefore perhaps most suitable, in *Delights for Ladies* by Sir Hugh Platt of the court of Elizabeth I. It was designed for enabling you to keep the flowers whole, so that there is no need to tear the petals off and discard the calixes; but of course when, as with most of these herbs, the leaves are as scented as the flowers, they are stripped from their stems. The flowers and leaves should be laid first carefully in a box on a bed of dry sand, with more sand between each layer. Sir Hugh then left the box in the sun, avoiding moisture and cooling, but for modern purposes you may use an airing cupboard, with the door left a crack ajar to allow moisture to escape lest evil spirits create a mould; it should be left there for twenty-one or let us say three times seven days, or nine times nine if the herbs are fleshy. The flowers and leaves will be found to have kept their shape and a memory of their colour as they dried.

The method was particularly intended for roses, whose beauty alone should allow us to count them among plants that 'comfort the heart',

even though they were never thought magical. But do not use modern varieties: hybrid teas, floribundas, and hybrid musks, however sweetly they smell when growing, do not hold their scent well when dried. Best of all are the old damasks, particularly the one usually marketed as Kazanlik, from which the famous attar of roses was made; the Red Rose of Lancaster (*gallica officinalis*, the apothecaries' rose) and the red cabbage rose, centifolia, come next; China and Bourbon roses, and the rugosas (which all have a hint of cloves in their scent), are excellent. All flowers and leaves for pot-pourri should be picked in the morning, when the sun has had time just to start volatising their essential oils, say by about eleven o'clock. Fixatives, always used in modern pot-pourri mixtures, are not really essential for this magical one; but if you like, for even longer life, add (when the other ingredients are dried) to a quart of them a tablespoon of powdered orris—which you can make yourself by drying the roots of white iris germanica very thoroughly for two or three months and grinding them. It has a scent of violets.

The mixture should be placed in a glass, porcelain or earthenware bowl, but by no means in one of silver or pewter, which the plants will dislike and tarnish in their ire with some trace of the essential oils which they have retained.

ORIGINAL
CONTRIBUTION
TO MAGIC

No book of this sort should fail to include at least one addition to magic lore. In keeping with our technological age, I contribute one for starting a motor mower. It is no use swearing at the machine, or invoking any of the demons potent in herbal magic—this has been tried. Attach to the handle a piece of fennel (for flattery, see Ben Jonson, *The Case Altered*, Act II, Scene 2), and then salute it with admiring words, saying it always starts at the first tug of its cleverly-designed cord; and assure anyone within earshot that it is the best machine on the market. And this, as the herbalists say, is sovereign.

INDEX